# Interview Questions

----- ✥❦✥ -----

*How To Nail That Worrisome Interview And Make That Dream Job A Reality*

**By Ronald Salem**

# Introduction

I want to thank you and congratulate you for joining me in my book, *"Interview Questions: How To Nail That Worrisome Interview And Make That Dream Job A Reality"*.

This book will help you look at interview details that most people overlook and aid you in gaining your confidence to conquer that up and coming interview.

By reading this book, you will not only get the best and professional advice to win an interview, but also how to finalize it and get your dream job. This book gives you the latest job interview trends, including preparing your outstanding portfolio and standing out during a focus group discussion.

At the end of the chapter, I will also guide you to double up your confidence so that your overall performance will be flawless and you can leave the interview room with no regret.

In all, this book is a perfect guide for first-time interviewees as well as those who want to improve their interview skills.

Thanks again for joining me here. Enjoy!

© **Copyright 2017. All rights reserved.**

This document is geared towards providing exact and reliable information in regards to the topic and issue covered. The publication is sold with the idea that the publisher is not required to render accounting, officially permitted, or otherwise, qualified services. If advice is necessary, legal or professional, a practiced individual in the profession should be ordered.

- From a Declaration of Principles which was accepted and approved equally by a Committee of the American Bar Association and a Committee of Publishers and Associations.

In no way is it legal to reproduce, duplicate, or transmit any part of this document in either electronic means or in printed format. Recording of this publication is strictly prohibited and any storage of this document is not allowed unless with written permission from the publisher. All rights reserved.

The information provided herein is stated to be truthful and consistent, in that any liability, in terms of inattention or otherwise, by any usage or abuse of any policies, processes, or directions contained within is the solitary and utter responsibility of the recipient reader. Under no circumstances will any legal responsibility or blame be held against the publisher for any reparation, damages, or monetary loss due to the information herein, either directly or indirectly.

Respective authors own all copyrights not held by the publisher.

The information herein is offered for informational purposes solely, and is universal as so. The presentation of the information is without contract or any type of guarantee assurance.

The trademarks that are used are without any consent, and the publication of the trademark is without permission or backing by the trademark owner. All trademarks and brands within this book are for clarifying purposes only and are the owned by the owners themselves, not affiliated with this document.

# Table of Contents

Introduction ............................................................................ 2

Chapter 1.  Interview Preparation Phase ................................ 6

Chapter 2.  General Interview Questions to Prepare ............ 10

Chapter 3.  Answering Tricky Questions .............................. 16

Chapter 4.  Portfolio: Your Added Values ............................ 20

Chapter 5.  Dealing With A Focus Group Discussion ............ 21

Chapter 6.  Boosting Your Confidence .................................. 24

Conclusion ............................................................................ 27

## Chapter 1.

# Interview Preparation Phase

No matter how many interviews you have attended earlier or how many of those you have won or lost, an interview is always a challenging event in your life. You will always have a nervous feeling because you never know what the company expects from you. Therefore, having an initial preparation before the interview is as important as the interview itself.

In this chapter, I will show you what things you need to do or acknowledge and what aspects you need to improve so that you can increase your opportunity to get your dream job.

**Your Look and Overall Appearance**

The term "Don't judge a book by its cover" is told to everyone as a child, but the truth is before other people know your real personalities and talents, they will first see your overall appearance. Thinking about how you look like during the interview is crucial because you will at least attract other people to be willing to see what you have.

If you are a man, make sure that you have trimmed your hair—including your facial hair—to make sure that your face looks clean. Wearing an appropriate outfit is also important to give a first impression of your professionalism.

If you are a woman, you have to think about your appearance in a more detailed manner. Not only what you wear, but you must also think about how you put your make-up—never put it on too heavy on your face.

Also, choose your outfit carefully and appropriately, including the length of your skirt and the heels of your shoes. Don't wear too much accessories and select simple designs for a more professional and cleaner look.

## Your Goals

Before you enter an interview room, you must also have to be certain about your goals. It means that you must have clear visions about your future, including short, medium, and long-term goals.

For companies, seeking the right candidates are more like finding the right personalities that match with the corporates' values. If your main intention to apply for a certain position is only money, the company may not respect that. Therefore, preparing answers for what your short, medium, and long term purposes are in your life is crucial to enable the recruiters to see your intentions.

Although you can make up answers, genuineness will be more appreciated because people in the HR positions are equipped with the ability to judge your true personalities from so many ways—including your gesture, eyeballs movement, intonation changes, facial expression, etc. That is the very reason why choosing a career based on your true passion is highly advisable because you will have more power to influence the interviewers that you are the right candidate for that position.

# Chapter 1. Interview Preparation Phase

## Your Knowledge of the Company

The next important thing to prepare is your basic knowledge of the company, including the history, values, target markets, products and services, etc. Internet is a great source to find important information about the company. First of all, you have to see the company's website. Then, you can search the news related to the company to see some current updates and issues that the company face.

"What do you know about this company?" is a typical interview question. Say some general facts that you know and add some detailed information (especially the positive ones) of the company.

## Your Knowledge of the Job Description

Aside from knowing the information about the company, you must also have the knowledge about what your duties and responsibilities are if you are offered the position. This kind of information will also help you to answer problem-solving questions that often appear in the interview.

The interviewers like to know your readiness, attitudes, and behaviors if you get the job and face some problems that may arise during your service. Such problem-solving questions are also used to see your real working values. Having the knowledge about your position and its job description will help you to give the appropriate answers.

## Your Gesture and Positive Tones

Other important aspects that you should train and prepare long before the interview are your positive gestures and tones. Too often, the interviewers give you tricky questions that may provoke you to reveal your negative attitudes or behaviors. To avoid unwanted incident in the interview room, you need to practice your positive reaction to every question.

For example, when you are asked about the reason why you left your previous company or what the most difficult situation you ever experienced, you must try to find the positive things behind even the worst circumstances. This will prevent you to display negative expression, intonations, or gestures. However, I personally recommend you to practice this skill over and over again until you can really control your response.

Once you prepare the things above, you are ready to move to the next phase. In the next chapters you will learn more about the interview questions and how to answer them effectively.

# Chapter 2.

# General Interview Questions to Prepare

There are several typical questions that are often asked during the job interview. In this chapter, I will show you what the questions are plus how to answer them. Please consider tailoring them based on your actual condition and personality so that your answers can reflect the real you. It is very important to keep in mind that honesty is the best policy in an interview.

By preparing some of the general interview questions, you can minimize your worrisome and be more prepared to face the interviewers. Here is the list of the most common questions in the interview room.

**Tell me about yourself?**

You should take this opportunity to show your communication skills by speaking clearly and concisely in an organized manner. Because there is no right or wrong answer for this question, it is important to appear friendly. Use your 2-3 minutes introduction time wisely.

As a suggestion, you may give some information about:

- Yourself: Name, nickname, place of origin, age, educational backgrounds: degree, university major, graduation time

- Your motivation to work for a company or a position

- Your qualification: major strengths, field of interests, previous experiences

- Your achievements you are most proud of

## What is your motivation to apply for this position or to work here?

Do thorough research about the position. Match it with the qualifications you have. Show your interest about the company and the position you are applying.

## What do you know about this company?

Do company research: history, products/services, target markets/customers, future plans, recent innovations, corporate cultures, etc., and try to find correlations between the information and your expertise.

## How will you contribute to this company?

This question is closely related to the previous question. Once you know a better and deeper understanding about the company, you can figure out what the company demands from you and the position you apply. A good and reputable company usually states a lot of information on its official website, including some recent news. Your job is to match the information with the set of skills and educational backgrounds

## Chapter 2. General Interview Questions to Prepare

you have. Assure them that you are the right candidate for the position by displaying humble, yet outstanding answers. You're your tone positive and confident because they are important indicators any interviewers are looking for in a candidate.

### What are your strengths?

Be carefully honest. Be confident, but don't sound too arrogant. Provide examples of your positive characteristics (how those positive things appear in real life situations). Prepare at least 3 answers and 2 other backups since this question may appear in many different forms (e.g. What you are good at? What kind of a person do you think you are? What make you a better candidate than other applicants? etc.). Providing backups will enable you not to state similar things over and over.

### Tell us about your achievements.

It could be your academic achievements or non-academic achievements (sports, arts, music, etc.). If you do not have any, you can mention simple things that were big contributions to your life. For example: When you defeated your fear and did your best to achieve your goals. Or, when you failed but then did not give up and gave your biggest efforts until you succeed.

### Tell us about your working experiences.

If you have any, be honest. Focus on the positive things. You can also tell them about your internships or part-time jobs. The idea is that they want to know whether or not you have the working ethos (to work individually or in a team, to work with high enthusiasm and discipline, to serve the company's values and interests, etc.).

# Interview Questions

The following question will be: So, why did you quit from the job?

You may answer that by saying you are looking for broader experiences and that the company and the position you are applying attract you better.

## Can you work under pressure? How do you handle pressure? Describe a situation in which you have to work under pressure.

Show your quality by saying "Yes", and provide an example from your past jobs or your college time when you were able to balance between your academic, organization, and other social and personal life well. Show them concrete evidence of your good scores, award certificates, organizational certificates, etc.

## How long will you stay with us? How long will you work for our company?

Do not say that you will only stay in the company for a short period of time, although maybe you will. Tell them that you will stay as long as your contribution is needed by the company. The company will never hire someone who does not take the job or the company seriously.

## What kind of life would you like to have in the next 3 or 5 or 10 years?

With this question, the interviewer wants to know about your short and long term goals. Be careful. Do not sound as if you are planning to leave the company as soon as your goals are accomplished or other better opportunities come ahead. However, you still have to show that you have clear vision about your life. So be wise in answering this question. Refer to

# Chapter 2. General Interview Questions to Prepare

the big pictures, do not state about specific careers if you plan to leave the company in a short period of time.

And also, be careful about your marriage plan.

**What is your philosophy towards work?**

Tell the interviewer, what kind of a worker are you (your positive qualities as a worker), the reason why you work, the passion you have toward the position or the company you are applying, etc. for example:

"I will work hard for my professional development as well as the development of the company."

"To work hard, to share and learn knowledge for and from the co-workers, to work sincerely and honestly, to apply what I have learnt for the benefit of many people, etc."

**What do you usually do in your leisure time?**

Tell them about your hobbies. Make it clear that your hobbies will not distract your concentration from your job, but will give valuable contribution to your job.

"I love playing tennis because it maintains my physical being as well as decreases my stress, so that I can return to my professional routine with new energy."

**How much do you expect if we offer this position to you?**

"I'm sure whatever I'm offered will be a fair price."

"I'm expecting somewhere between $... - $...."

"I know that the average pay for this position is roughly around $..., but because I have a couple years more experience, I would want something around $.... to $...."

Please note that in a final interview, salary negotiation will possibly happen. So, make sure you do a research about the average salary in a certain position/location.

## What have you done to improve your capacities, knowledge, or yourself?

Give examples including trainings, seminars, conferences, workshops, peer learning, supervisor-subordinate learning, self-learning, etc.

## Tell me about your family.

Don't say too much about your family. Moreover, don't use it as a sharing time. Tell what is necessary to tell and make sure you add the positive thing you gain for being a member of your family.

"I am the first son in the family, and I have three siblings. This makes me a responsible and reliable person since I have to take care of my little brothers and sister and my parents demand me to always be good examples for them."

"I am raised in a family who is concerned about education. I am thankful for my family who has always been supportive to each other, making us become positive and optimistic people."

# Chapter 3.

# Answering Tricky Questions

Beware that some questions asked during the interview session are quite tricky, in which they want to dig deeper about the real quality you have as an individual and as a professional worker.

## Don't Get Trapped With Negative Questions

When the interviewers ask you negative questions, do not focus on the negative aspects. Instead, try to find the positive sides of those negativities. Here are some examples of negative questions.

*What are your weaknesses? What is the worst failure you have had in life? Have you ever experienced a hardship in your life?*

Be careful in answering these questions. The most important thing is not the weakness, failure, or hardship that you have, but the lesson learnt you take from those negative things. Show to your prospectus employer that you have tried hard to or are in the process of eliminating or at least decreasing the negative aspects of yourself.

# Interview Questions

You may also refer to your past failure that you have overcome.

**Tip**: Make your weakness becomes your positive value/strength.

## Shifting Negative Aspects into Positive Ones

When answering negative questions, you must shift the negative aspects into positive ones.

Follow this basic rule:

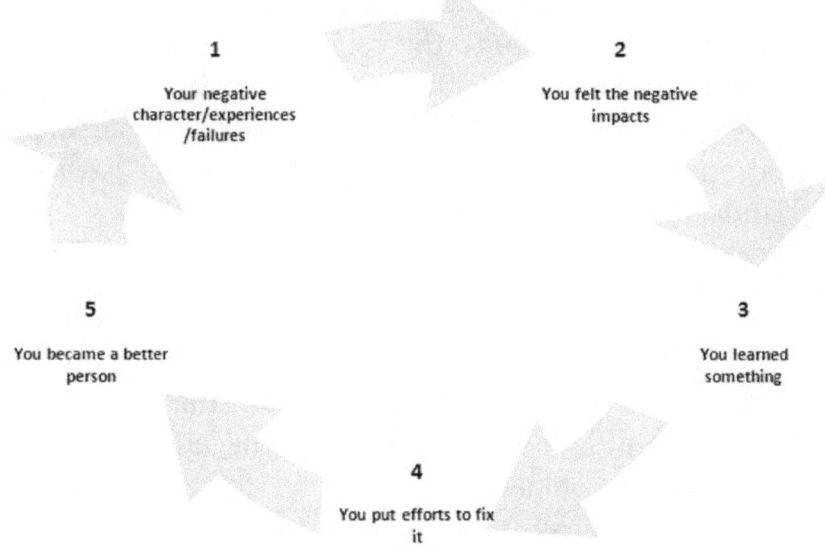

## Other examples of tricky questions

### Why haven't you found a position before now?

You can say that you are not only looking for any job, but the one that really suits your qualification, characteristics, passion, and goals. Then tell them about your dream job.

## Chapter 3. Answering Tricky Questions

Or, if you have a reasonable real answer, state it. For example, you want to pursue your dream to go around the world to learn about diversity, or you want to join a certain training, etc.

Never state negative things like "I've applied to many jobs but I haven't heard from them," or "I failed in several other interviews, I wasn't lucky enough."

### *Do you know anyone who works for us?*

Be careful in answering this question. Some companies may have a policy for not allowing two people who share blood or marriage relationship to work in the same place. Moreover, you do not know whether the person that you mention has good image or contribution to the company or not. Therefore, it is important to know about the company's policy. If you just know someone, simply say "I know A from xxx department, but we are not that close," or just say "No, I don't have any close friends or relation who works here."

### *What irritates you about co-workers?*

I can work with anyone and any type of person. However, I prefer those who are honest rather than those who are deceitful. The point is: do not focus on the negative sides, but more on the positive points.

### *Tell me about your dream job?*

Be careful, this question is related to the question: How long will you stay or work for this company. It is better to say that the position you are applying will lead you to a higher position that you are dreaming of. Remember that it is important to give an impression that you plan to work for a long time in the company and build your career there.

## *Are you applying for other jobs?*

Tell the truth. However, show them that the company attracts you more and become your first priority since you have passion to work in the position and that your characteristics suit the position and the values of the company.

Chapter 4.

# Portfolio: Your Added Values

Another good way to kill your anxiety and nail the interview down is by creating a good portfolio that you can bring during the interview session. You can show this portfolio at the end of the interview so that they will consider it when they discuss and decide who will be eligible for the position.

Your portfolio is the extended version of your curriculum vitae. It contains some samples of your masterpieces. It could be in a form of written documents, summary of publications, pictures, videos, and other files that may distinguish you from other applicants.

You can create a digital and/or printed portfolio. However, the most important thing is **to explain and show** a glimpse of your portfolio to catch their attention and willingness to read or take a look at it. Without that effective explanation, they will simply put it in the trash.

Chapter 5.

# Dealing With A Focus Group Discussion

A focus group discussion is also called a panel discussion or a group discussion. Many companies use this kind of an interview strategy to short out qualified candidates quickly. Moreover, this kind of strategy is very useful if the company wants to reveal the true characteristics of the job applicants.

Small group of people will be invited to join the discussion. The interviewer will provide a topic for you to discuss. Usually, they will analyze your personalities and whether your characteristics suit to the culture that the company has. Usually, the topic appeared in the discussion is a current issue, so that it is important for a job applicant to always keep up with the current issues. Another possible topic is job or position-related topic. So, it is also important to do company research and keep up with the current trends. For example, marketing strategy if you are applying a position as a marketer or technology if you are applying a position that concerning technology development.

# Chapter 5. Dealing With A Focus Group Discussion

There are several tips in facing a focus group discussion:

1. **Take role as a moderator/initiator.**

   This will give you an advantage as a pioneer. The interviewer will get an impression that you have a leadership quality. It can also give you an advantage in which you will maintain your position as a middle man who will keep your objectivity in a discussion. It will also keep you away for being too judgmental.

2. **Take role as a dispute resolver and problem solver**

   When the discussion is getting too intense, the moderator sometimes loose his/her function and objectivity. It is time for you to be a dispute resolver. Present the negative and positive side equally so that the people can digest the problems wisely.

3. **'Take over' the moderator's role**

   When the moderator seems to get confused about what to do or with the opinion of the rest member of the group, you can 'take over' the moderator's role politely by restating again the case/topic and then give a quick review of the discussion.

   If the discussion is not focus, you can take over the moderator's role by directing the discussion back into its original topic.

## Interview Questions

4.  **Take the role as a decision maker**

    The time given for a discussion is limited. Sometimes, the moderator does not pay attention to the time and simply lets the discussion flow. You can jump in the discussion by concluding the whole discussion and try to give the best solution for the problem.

5.  **If you don't have the opportunity to be one of the roles above, you still can catch the interview's attention by stating something that is 'out of the box'.** It is somehow difficult, but give yourself a try.

6.  **Do not say something that is too general.** It will make you 'invisible'. Your effort won't be noted, and worse, people will think you are nothing. However, if you can present the general opinion with good explanation so that people will see the effectiveness of your solution, go ahead.

7.  **Present your opinion in the mild manner.** Don't be too stubborn. It will give an impression that you are not able to listen and are not open minded.

8.  **Do not attack your opponent so harshly.** Present your disagreement strongly but politely.

9.  **Focus to the question.** If you are asked about solutions, give solutions. Do not focus on the problems only.

10. **Speak with good and positive attitudes.**

Chapter 6.

# Boosting Your Confidence

At the end of this book, I am sure that you have gained more confidence to face the upcoming interview. Remember that in the interview, it is not merely about the interviewers who want to know more about you and find out whether or not your qualities suit to the company's requirements. How well you know yourself and how certain you are that you are the right person for the candidate is a lot more important. You won't believe how your confidence of being you can influence other people to trust and finally choose you.

To sum up, you need to do the following:

1. Define your own purpose or goals in your life, including the reason why you work and apply to the particular position in the particular company. Make it as your ultimate reasons to get the job.

2. Be sure that you will only apply to something that you really love to do. This will double up your confidence.

3. Rehearse the interview questions over and over. Make up some position-related and also technical questions. Invite other people to critique you.

## Interview Questions

4. Train your body language in front of the mirror. Loot at your own posture and see your gestures. Improve the things that you think are lacking and eliminate the things you don't like.

5. Try your interview outfit before the D-day. Make sure that you feel comfortable with whatever you wear or use.

6. Try to eat something to give you energy before the interview.

7. Drink water. Be aware that coffee or tea will make you even more nervous if you don't get used to caffeine. Never consume alcohol before the interview.

8. Prepare your portfolio, in the form of digital files or printed doc (or both)

9. Bring important documents that may be asked before or during the interview session.

10. No excessive make up, fragrance, etc.

11. Take a deep breath. Remember that you have prepared everything.

12. Don't get intimidated by other candidates. Focus on yourself and your strengths.

13. Always make eye contact with the interviewers.

# Chapter 6. Boosting Your Confidence

14. Keep your mind positive because positivity will give you good energy. If you think positively, you can make it easier to behave and speak in positive manners.

15. Do your best.

# Conclusion

Thanks again for reading my book!

I hope this book was able to help you learn more about small details that will make you stand out from the rest and magnify your chances of scoring that job you've always wanted.

The next step is to walk into that interview room and let them know why you are just the person for the job!

Finally, if you enjoyed this book, then I'd like to ask you for a favor, would you be kind enough to leave a review for this book on Amazon? It'd be greatly appreciated!

Thank you and good luck!

Conclusion

www.ingramcontent.com/pod-product-compliance
Lightning Source LLC
Chambersburg PA
CBHW061240180526
45170CB00003B/1379